Beneath the Sea

IN 3-D

by

MARK BLUM

CHRONICLE BOOKS

SAN FRANCISCO

Water photograph on the cover and
pages 1, 2, and 5 by Leon Garden.

Manufactured in China.

ISBN: 0-8118-1412-2

Library of Congress Cataloging-in-
Publication Data available.

Editing: Kay Kirby
Design: Dennis Gallagher and John
Sullivan, Visual Strategies,
San Francisco

Distributed in Canada by
Raincoast Books
9050 Shaughnessy Street
Vancouver, B.C. V6P 6E5

10 9 8 7 6 5 4

Chronicle Books LLC
85 Second Street
San Francisco, California 94105

www.chroniclebooks.com

Preface

I was fifteen years old when I first held in my hands that odd-looking camera at the neighbor's garage sale. It wasn't shaped like a camera, and it had too many lenses, but I had to have it anyway. When I brought it home, my father showed me what the Stereo Realist could do. I was astounded—the camera took three-dimensional pictures. Those mesmerizing illusions of reality held my young imagination for countless hours.

A decade after catching the stereophotography bug, I developed a similar passion for scuba diving. More than anything, I was fascinated by the strange and beautiful creatures living beneath the surface of the sea. I quickly took up underwater photography in hopes of recording their likenesses and behavior.

Several years passed before I realized that it must be possible to photograph underwater in 3-D. My first experiments, shot through the windows of aquariums, were stunning. Stereophotography seemed ideally suited to the detailed, colorful, underwater environment. The promise of those early photographs inspired my search for methods to shoot in stereo while scuba diving. This book chronicles the results of my obsession.

On the following pages you will encounter marine life ranging from sweeping schools of fish to minuscule shrimp. Through the magic of stereophotography, even veteran divers and biologists will experience many creatures as they have never seen them before. When you view the diminutive Gaudy clown crab, for example, it will appear a virtual leviathan. This effect occurs because the twin lenses of the unique cameras used to produce this work are spaced much closer together than the 2 1/2 inches between human pupils. As a result, you will observe the remarkable three-dimensional detail of the crab as another member of its species would see it, as if your eyes were only 5/32 of an inch apart!

The stereophotographs collected here consist of two images taken from two different perspectives. When the two halves of the stereo pair are merged in the visual cortex, our computerlike brains reassemble the data into a single image with the perception of depth.

Most underwater photography takes place within three feet of the subject. In 3-D, these short distances require cameras with relatively small separations ("stereo base") between the lenses. The nearer the subject, the closer together the lenses must be. Although factory-built 3-D cameras from the stereo heyday of the 1950s are still easy to find (especially the Stereo Realist), their standard 2 1/2-inch lens separation is unsuitable for the vast majority of underwater subjects. To compound the problem, very few production stereo cameras are manufactured today, and none have been designed specifically for underwater use. Aspiring underwater "stereographers" are therefore required to build or adapt their own underwater 3-D camera systems.

The photographs in this work were taken with five stereo camera systems, all of which were custom designed and specially built or modified for a particular photographic challenge. One appears to have the unusual distinction of being the world's only single-lens reflex, medium-format, macro stereo camera. The lenses of these cameras are spaced from 2mm to 38mm apart. Two of the camera systems are based on a single Nikonos camera body, while the others incorporate custom stereo cameras in underwater housings. Images are produced in 18 x 24mm, 24 x 36mm and 30 x 45mm film formats.

This book is a collection of journeys beneath the surface of the world's oceans. As you venture through it, you will visit many unique environments: the quiet heart of a kelp forest off the California coast; coral reefs surrounding the South Pacific islands of Fiji and Borneo; marine parks of various Caribbean islands; and vibrant blue waters lapping the stark shores of Baja California. These extraordinary places sustain some of the most fascinating creatures on earth. It is my hope that you will share my wonderment as you view them for the first time through the close-set "eyes" of the stereo camera.

The Plates

Stoplight Parrotfish

LITTLE CAYMAN ISLAND, CARIBBEAN *SPARISOMA VIRIDE*

The Stoplight parrotfish is one of many species that undergo dramatic changes in shape and appearance as they mature. These phases are designated juvenile, adult, and supermale. This specimen is a supermale, the largest and most colorful phase of the parrotfish's development. The stout beak of the parrotfish is used to scrape algae from the reef. In the grazing process, coral is ingested in large quantities. Later, it is excreted over the reef, making parrotfish the most important producers of tropical sand. A few species of parrotfish secrete mucous cocoons, which may block their scent from eels and other nocturnal hunters, while they sleep. At night, parrotfish settle in sheltered places to sleep and are easy to photograph quite closely. This fish slumbered unperturbed through a dozen brilliant flash exposures.

Nudibranch *NEMBROTHA CRISTATA*

SIPADAN ISLAND, BORNEO, MALAYSIA

Nudibranchs are shell-less marine snails. Lacking the defensive protection of a shell, most species arm themselves with toxins or stinging cells borrowed from the animals they feed on. This specimen is dining on tunicates. In order to reach the tunicates' soft insides, the Nudibranch scrapes through the tough outer tube with a ribbon of teeth known as a radula. When I took this picture, I did not notice the two miniature crabs hiding in the coral.

Reef Octopus *OCTOPUS BRIAREUS*

COZUMEL ISLAND, MEXICO

The bottom-dwelling octopus is behaviorally the most complex invertebrate in the world, with highly sophisticated senses of vision and touch. Pigment cells in the skin (chromatophores) allow for rapid color changes that serve to camouflage the animal and allow it to communicate with other members of its species. Males die after mating. After laying her eggs, the female octopus will spend the next several months guarding and cleaning them to the exclusion of all else—including feeding herself. This valiant effort usually proves fatal, however, with death claiming the female shortly after the young have hatched.

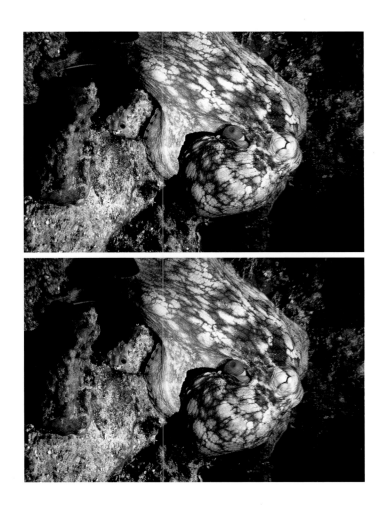

Queen Angelfish *HOLACANTHUS CILIARIS*

COZUMEL ISLAND, MEXICO

Few fish match the beauty and grace of the angelfish. The Queen angelfish is particularly striking, with a speckled blue crown on its forehead. As with most reef fish, the distinctive color pattern is important for species recognition and social rank. Most angelfish live in harems, in which the males defend a territory containing two or more females while driving away male rivals. Although generally warier than other common Caribbean angelfish species, with careful stalking the Queen angelfish may be approached closely.

Giant Clam *TRIDACNA GIGAS*

These huge clams are the world's biggest bivalves, reaching nearly five feet in length and weighing up to 650 pounds. Their long lives may span a century or more. The beautiful coloration of the multi-hued mantle is caused in part by oxygen-producing algae (*zooxanthellae*) growing within the tissues of the clam. The symbiotic algae use sunlight to synthesize carbon, which in turn feeds the host clam. Several animals, such as shrimp and various goby species, have a similar commensal relationship with the clam, where their presence neither harms nor benefits the host. They are often found living in the mantle or siphon tubes of the Giant clam.

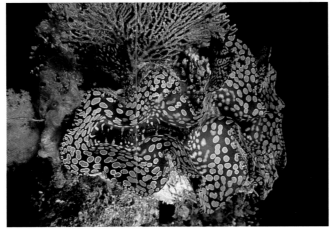

Tiger Grouper *MYCTEROPERCA TIGRIS*

LITTLE CAYMAN ISLAND, CARIBBEAN

These members of the sea bass family (Serranidae), with their stocky bodies, large mouths, and jutting lower jaws, are voracious predators of fish and crustaceans. Unwary prey are sucked into the grouper's gullet when it snaps open its great mouth. The catch is held fast by the sharp teeth (evident in the photograph), then swallowed whole. Individuals of some larger grouper species may be several decades old. Their curiosity, appetite, and bottom-dwelling habits render them especially vulnerable to depletion in overfished areas.

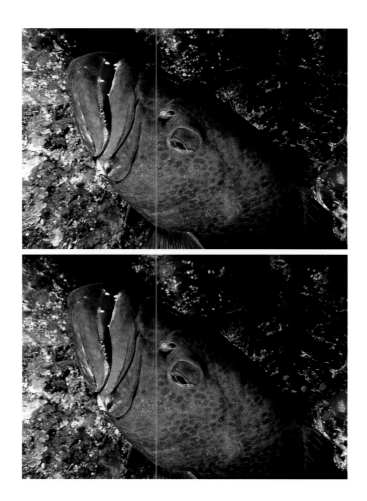

Blackfin Barracuda *SPHYRAENA GENIE*

SIPADAN ISLAND, BORNEO, MALAYSIA

The barracuda is an aggressive predator of other fish, but rarely attacks humans. All species possess large mouths and long knifelike teeth. This particular species attains a length of more than three feet. During the day, Blackfin barracuda are often found schooling by the thousands in the strong currents swirling off the points of tropical islands. Swimming in the midst of perhaps a thousand barracudas, I felt as if the school were a single huge organism.

Anemone Shrimp *PERICLIMENES YUCATANICUS*
in Giant Anemone *CONDYLACTIS GIGANTEA*

COZUMEL ISLAND, MEXICO

This uniquely patterned Anemone shrimp is living in the tentacles of its usual host, the Giant anemone, but members of the species also may make their homes in Branching or Corkscrew anemones. The relationship of shrimp to anemone is commensal, or symbiotic: The shrimp neither harms nor benefits its host and is immune to its stings. Every delicate feature of this tiny shrimp, about .8 inches long, is revealed with the aid of macro stereophotography.

Peppered Moray Eel *SIDEREA PICTA*

SIPADAN ISLAND, BORNEO, MALAYSIA

The Peppered moray makes its daytime home in crevices but at night forages anywhere on the reef. This specimen is framed by *Galaxea* coralheads. The many sharp teeth, set in a powerful jaw, can cause severe lacerations to a diver's hands. Although the fangs are not venomous, they are often coated with a poisonous mucous, making infection from bites common. Some morays are edible, but most are oily and unpalatable. The flesh of a few species is poisonous.

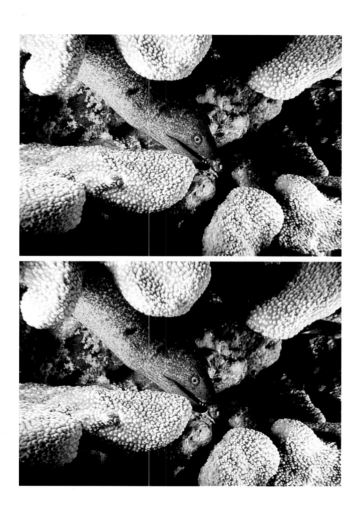

Christmas Tree Worm *SPIROBRANCHUS GIGANTEUS*

The Christmas tree worm derives its common name from the appearance of its delicate spiral branches protruding from a tube within the coral. The slightest change in light or current causes the worm to instantly retract, pulling a "trapdoor" shut behind it. The door, or operculum, is armored with a sharp spine to discourage predators. Such highly successful evasive tactics can be equally discouraging to underwater photographers. Stalking the worms with a lens requires great patience and a few tricks. For example, often one worm in a group is not sensitive. When this worm is located by waving one's arms over the field of worms, the photographer has found a very cooperative subject indeed.

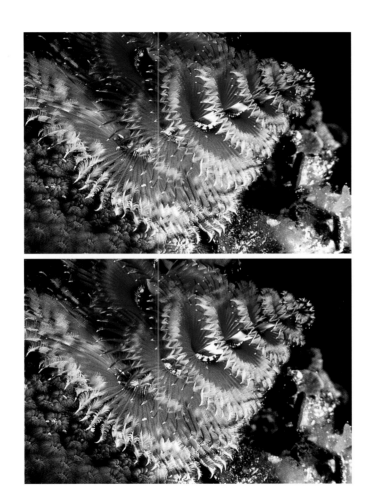

Margate

HAEMULON ALBUM

Margates belong to the large Grunt family of fishes found in warm shallow seas around the world. The common family name comes from the distinctive "grunting" sound that the fish generates by rubbing together the tooth plates in its throat and then amplifying the sound in the air bladder. This generally shy species can be found alone or in small schools. A distinctive feature of the Margate is the presence of scales between the mouth and the gills. It is also the largest member of the Grunt family, reaching more than two feet.

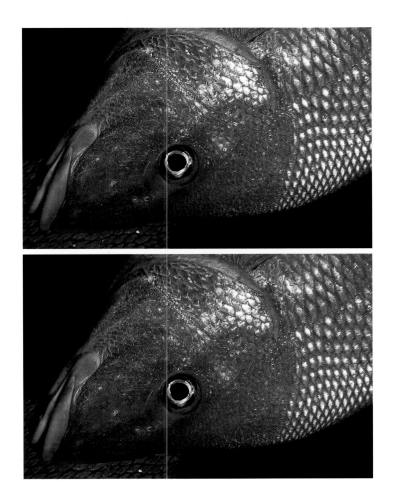

Thorny Oyster *SPONDYLUS SP.*

SIPADAN ISLAND, BORNEO, MALAYSIA

The exterior of this bivalve is encrusted with algae, sponges, and even solitary cup coral, with its yellow polyps extended. Short tentacles, which act as taste organs, ring the shell amid dozens of eyes. Sensing my approach, this oyster has already drawn closed its surrealistic mantle. Behind it lie the elaborate gills that filter tiny plants and animals from the current normally flowing through. A distinctive Banded coral shrimp (*Stenopus hispidus*) waits in the foreground for a fish to clean.

Bulb-Tentacle Sea Anemone *ENTACMAEA QUADRICOLOR*
with Spine-cheek Anemonefish *PREMNAS BIACULEATUS*

SIPADAN ISLAND, BORNEO, MALAYSIA

The mechanism that provides anemonefish immunity against the stinging cells of their host anemones is not yet fully understood, but it is likely a combination of biochemistry and behavior. This is the solitary form of the Bulb-tentacle sea anemone. Although this anemone species plays host to thirteen different species of anemonefish, the Spine-cheek anemonefish lives only in the Bulb-tentacle sea anemone.

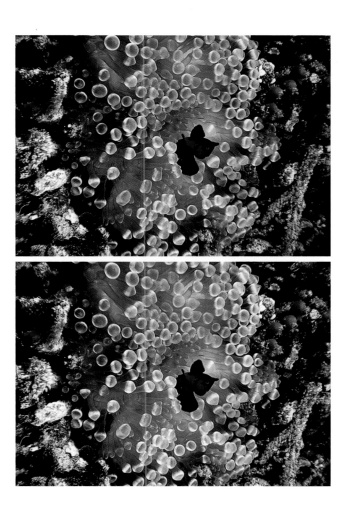

Pederson's Cleaning Shrimp
and Corkscrew Anemone

PERICLIMENES PEDERSONI

BARTHOLOMEA ANNULATA

LITTLE CAYMAN ISLAND, CARIBBEAN

This delicate shrimp is a cleaner, ridding fish hosts of parasites and fungi. Its cleaning station is the Corkscrew anemone. Like the anemonefish and a few other reef creatures, the shrimp develops an immunity to the anemone's stinging nematocysts. The Pederson's cleaning shrimp advertises its services by waving its delicate white antenna at passing fish. Secure in the importance of its function, this tiny shrimp ventures fearlessly into the mouths of ferocious predators, normally returning unscathed. The shrimp also will frequently clean the hand of a diver, if offered.

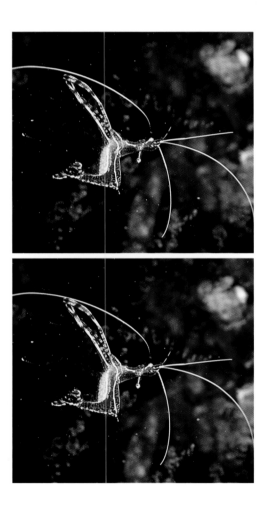

Sharpnose Puffer *CANTHIGASTER ROSTRATA*

LITTLE CAYMAN ISLAND, CARIBBEAN

Pufferfish are named for their ability to puff up their bodies by drawing water into a special chamber—one of several defense mechanisms designed to deter predators. In addition, the pufferfish's skin and viscera contain tetrodotoxin. This powerful poison has killed many people who have eaten pufferfish flesh but does not always have the same effect on predatory fish. Species of *Canthigaster* supplement their toxicity with a secretion from their skin to further discourage animals from preying on them.

Schoolmaster *LUTJANUS APODUS*

These fish are members of the snapper family. The common name "snapper" derives from the fish's jaw-snapping reaction to being caught on a hook. The color of fish in this species varies, but the fins are always a distinctive yellow. Also note the blue line under the eye and the pale bar pattern. The Schoolmaster is wary and sometimes difficult to approach closely. This pair is framed by Star coral on the left and Brain coral on the right. An adult Stoplight parrotfish appears in the background.

Hermit Crab PAGURUS ARMATUS

MONTEREY BAY, CALIFORNIA

This crab is one of thirty thousand species forming the class Crustacea, containing crabs, shrimp, lobsters and other obscure forms. The Hermit crab is recognized by its habit of borrowing the discarded homes of other animals, most commonly an empty snail shell. As the crab outgrows its home, it will move to successively larger residences. Most species are scavengers, feeding off plant and animal debris. The Hermit crab occupies habitats from the intertidal zone to the darkness twelve hundred feet below.

Green Sea Turtle

CHELONIA MYDAS

Sea turtles belong to an exclusive group of just forty marine reptile species. The sea turtle is dependent upon land only to provide a beach nesting site for its eggs. Coming ashore after sundown, the female Green Sea turtle struggles up the beach to dig a hole safely above the high tide line. She deposits dozens of leathery eggs in the nest and then buries them under two to three feet of sand. The laborious process can last all night. After a month of incubation deep beneath the warm beach, young Green Sea turtles simultaneously begin to hatch out of their shells and claw their way to the surface. They usually emerge at night in order to avoid predators such as birds, reptiles, and fish as they make their way instinctively back to the open sea. When the females are ready to lay their eggs, four to six years later, they return to the very same beach where they were hatched.

Whitetip Soldierfish *MYRIPRISTIS VITTATA*

SIPADAN ISLAND, BORNEO, MALAYSIA

Soldierfish are part of the large Holocentridae family, which also includes squirrelfish. Nocturnally active, soldierfish are reef-dwelling fish and feed on zooplankton above the reef. Daylight typically finds aggregations of Whitetip soldierfish sheltering in caves along the deeper part of the outer reef, where their large eyes are well adapted to dim light. Many species of soldierfish look similar, usually with red coloration. This widely distributed species is most easily recognized by the white tips on its dorsal spine and the lack of a distinctively colored operculum bar along the edge of the gill cover.

Scrawled Filefish *ALUTERUS SCRIPTUS*

LITTLE CAYMAN ISLAND, CARIBBEAN

The filefish comprise a large family (Monacanthidae) of approximately one hundred species and are found in every ocean. They are closely related to triggerfish but have the ability to change color to match their surroundings. Many filefish species also change shape as they mature. Young filefish tend to be circular and compressed, becoming elongated as adults. Juvenile filefish are pelagic, meaning that they live in the open sea, floating with weeds, sometimes in schools. Adults are generally solitary but occasionally are seen in pairs or groups. The bizarre-looking Scrawled filefish is found in all tropical seas, drifting over coral reefs. It feeds on a variety of marine organisms, including algae, anemones, hydrozoans, gorgonians, seaweed, and tunicates.

False Clown Anemonefish *AMPHIPRION OCELLARIS*
with Magnificent Sea Anemone *HETERACTIS MAGNIFICA*

SIPADAN ISLAND, BORNEO, MALAYSIA

The anemonefish is a poor swimmer and relies on the protection of the anemone, with which it is invariably found. This scene, with a mated pair and two to four smaller fish, represents a typical social structure. If the larger, socially dominant female is removed from the anemone, the male of the pair becomes a female, and another male assumes his function. The smaller fish in the picture are not necessarily young—their growth is stunted by an aggressive hierarchy, which keeps them fleeing from the attacks of larger fish.

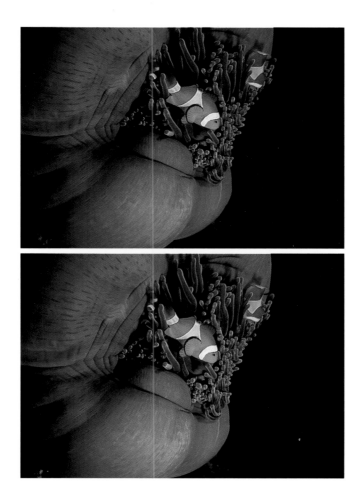

Spiny Lobster *PANULIRUS ARGUS*

Despite its sharp-spined armor, the lobster is a shy creature that travels and hunts by night. During the day it hides in recesses with only its long, sensitive antennae protruding. This lobster is using its antennae to "feel" the camera, which invaded its lair. Lobsters can also produce an alarming sound, somewhat like the sound of rosin being rubbed against a violin string, by scraping their antennae against ridges on their shells. In order to reach full size, lobsters must regularly molt their rigid exoskeleton. This is accomplished by partly absorbing the calcium from the old shell while a new exoskeleton begins to form beneath it. Some tropical Pacific species of lobsters are toxic, but human poisonings are rare.

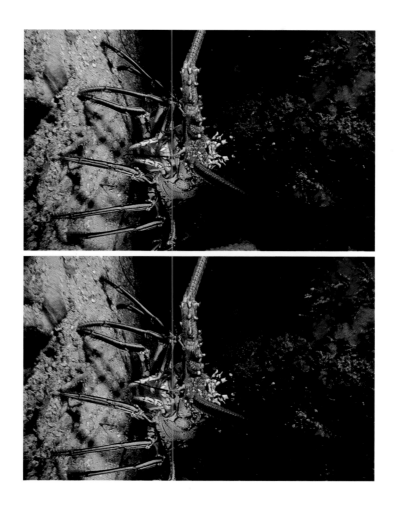

Sailfin Blenny

EMBLEMARI PANDIONIS

LITTLE CAYMAN ISLAND, CARIBBEAN

These small, shy fish live in holes, where they are often overlooked by divers. Most of the time only the head protrudes, as photographed here. When a particle of food floats by, the blenny darts out to retrieve it and flashes its sail-like fin several times. In an instant it retreats, tail first, into its hole. This extreme macro stereophoto shows the minute detail of the blenny's fingernail-sized head, including the fleshy appendages, or cirrus, growing above the eyes and on the snout.

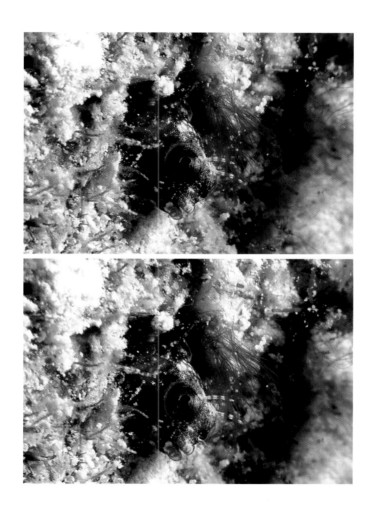

Red Bigeye

PRIACANTHUS CRUENTATUS

All members of this small family (Priacanthidae) have the very large eyes from which their name derives. Normally sheltered and solitary during the day, bigeyes often gather at night before migrating into open water to feed. Despite their large mouths, they favor small animals such as the larvae of crabs, shrimp, and fish. Daytime coloration is generally red, changing to silvery patterns at night. Most species are deepwater dwellers, but the Red bigeye inhabits shallower lagoons and reefs.

Purple Jellyfish

PELAGIA PANOPYRA

CARMEL BAY, CALIFORNIA

Seen from below, the dangling tentacles of the Purple jellyfish contain poisonous stinging cells used to stun prey. Here, young crabs have taken up temporary residence beneath the dome-shaped medusa, or bell. The Medusafish (*Icichthys lockingtoni*) is sometimes known to share a symbiotic relationship with this jellyfish, drifting together in the ocean currents.

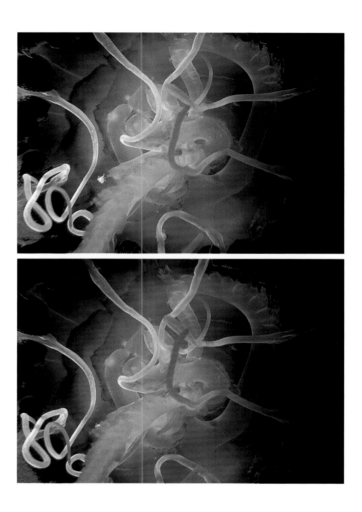

Gaudy Clown Crab

PLATYPODIELLA SPECTABILIS

LITTLE CAYMAN ISLAND, CARIBBEAN

This aptly named character inhabits shallow sand and coral rubble patches. Despite its minute proportions—its carapace measures only $1/4$ to $3/4$ of an inch across—the Gaudy clown crab is relatively fearless. A true crab, it is a member of the Xanthidae, or dark-fingered crab family. Careful and patient observation of crabs can be rewarding, because they often engage in elaborate courtship behavior. The female carries the eggs beneath her abdomen on special appendages. After the crab larvae hatch, they pass through several larval stages before settling on the bottom and assuming adult form.

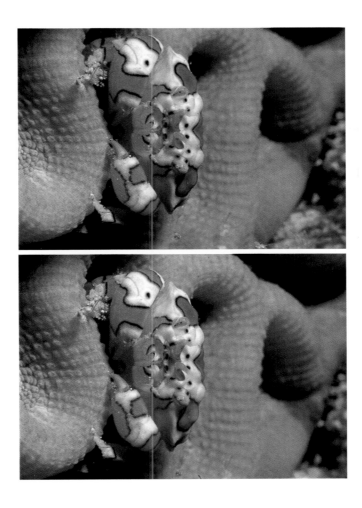

Sea Turtle Skeleton *CHELONIA MYDAS*

SIPADAN ISLAND, BORNEO, MALAYSIA

Beneath Sipidan Island, off Borneo, lies a deep, labyrinthine cavern, where this turtle and others like it have met macabre deaths. Nearby are the skeletons of a dolphin and a marlin that suffered similar fates. It appears that turtles and other large animals enter the cavern, become lost in the darkness and drown. Even with dive lights, I found the intricately chambered cave highly disorienting. When I turned my lights off in the deep recess and imagined being lost there, it was truly terrifying.

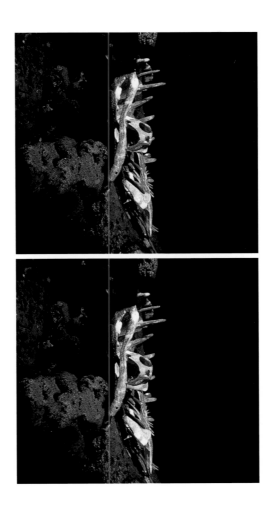

Nassau Grouper *EPINEPHELUS STRIATUS*

LITTLE CAYMAN ISLAND, CARIBBEAN

Here a grouper enjoys a frequent stop at a cleaning station, while a Pederson's cleaning shrimp picks parasites from its gills. A pair of gobyfish, not visible in the photograph, cleaned inside the grouper's mouth. Stereophotography provides a unique interior view of the fish's huge palate. The single antenna protruding from the corner of its mouth is all that remains of a Spiny lobster. Nassau groupers are often curious and approachable. This specimen followed me around the reef for nearly an hour, placing itself in my path at every opportunity.

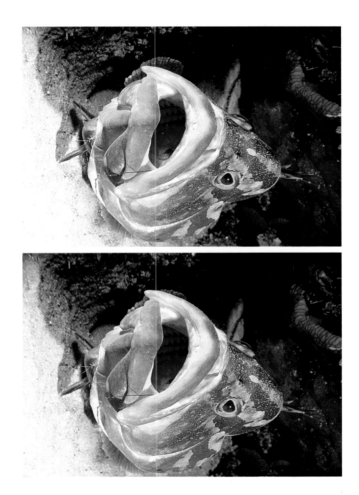

Soft Coral *DENDRONEPHTHYA SP.*

KANDAVU ISLAND, FIJI

Soft corals do not build a solid skeleton around their polyps as do the hard, or true, corals. Instead, they have internal skeletal fragments, crystals of calcium carbonate, which are not fused together. This difference makes the coral flexible and soft to the touch. Stinging cells in the polyps subdue and hold onto plankton before passing it down to the mouth. Scuba divers are drawn to the incredible rainbow of colors exhibited by soft corals. Upon closer examination, other animals are often found living in close association with the coral, such as the Hermit crabs pictured here.

Majestic Lionfish *PTEROIS VOLITANS*

SIPADAN ISLAND, BORNEO, MALAYSIA

The spectacular lionfish is among the most beautiful of all coral reef fish. Vividly contrasting coloration warns predators away from its highly venomous spines. Daylight typically finds the lionfish sheltering in shallow water crevices or under ledges. As night falls, it ventures out to feed on small fish and crustaceans. Clever carnivores, lionfish sometimes herd smaller fish into a trap with the deft manipulation of plumelike pectoral fins. Lionfish are not camera shy and are particularly easy to photograph at night. This fish followed me along the reef, preying on small fish that were dazed by the unexpected luminescence of my dive lights.

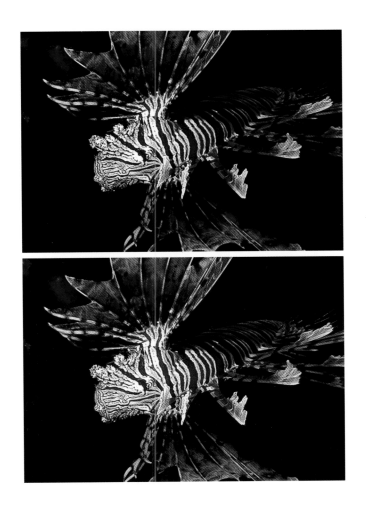

Yellowhead Jawfish *OPISTOGNATHUS AURIFRONS*

LITTLE CAYMAN ISLAND, CARIBBEAN

These curious fish are one of approximately seventy species in the family Opistognathidae. Here the Yellowhead is photographed expelling sand as it excavates a vertical burrow near the reef. It reinforces the well-like hole with bits of rock or coral. The males incubate the eggs of young jawfish in their mouths. They are often found hovering partly in or over their burrows, feeding on passing zooplankton. When frightened, they retreat tail first into the burrow.

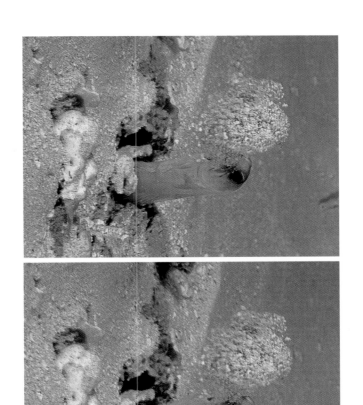

Cylinder Sea Anemone

SIPADAN ISLAND, BORNEO, MALAYSIA

CERIANTHUS FILIFORMIS

Tube anemones have a specialized, leathery tube for burrowing in sand. At the first sign of danger, they quickly draw down into their shelter. Tube anemones capture plankton and other small animals with their long, stinging tentacles. A mucous coating helps the anemone retain the food as it is passed to the central mouth. The Cylinder sea anemone, and several other species in this family, reportedly can cause remarkably painful stings in humans. This specimen was photographed on the dim floor of the "turtle tomb" beneath Sipidan Island.

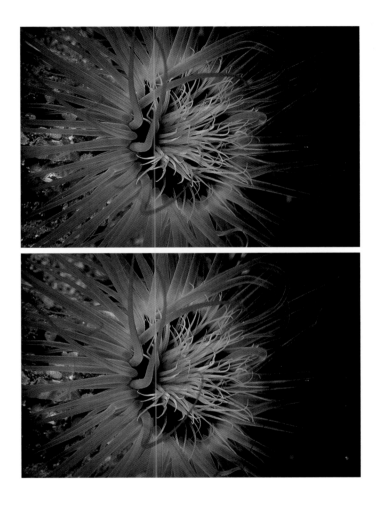

Peacock Flounder

BOTHUS LUNATUS

LITTLE CAYMAN ISLAND, CARIBBEAN

The exposed side of this flat-bodied fish is covered with brilliant blue rings and spots. Despite its beautiful patterning, the Peacock flounder easily blends into the sandy bottom by changing its tone and color. Undulating across the bottom like a wave, this carnivore feeds on small crustaceans and fish. Although both stalklike eyes of the adult flounder are on the left side of the head, they don't start out that way: Juvenile flounders adapt to swimming with one side against the bottom. In the process, one eye migrates over the head to the other side.

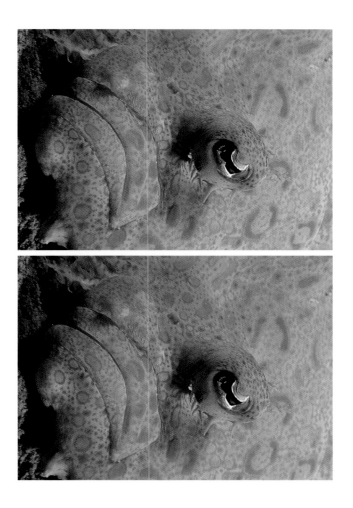

Fairy Basslet *PSEUDANTHIAS SP.*

KANDAVU ISLAND, FIJI

Small, colorful Fairy basslets are typically found on steep outer reef slopes. They congregate around coral heads or overhangs, feeding on tiny zooplankton. When danger threatens, and at night, basslets shelter within the complex reef. Often one or more males inhabit the territory of numerous, slightly less resplendent females. The brilliantly hued males put on an aggressive territorial display with erect fins and may change color rapidly. All males are actually sexually reversed females. If there are no males in the territory, the dominant female changes sex in order to assure continued breeding, through a developmental process known as sequential hermaphroditism.

Gopher Rockfish *SEBASTES CARNATUS*
and Strawberry Anemones *CORYNACTIS CALIFORNICA*

MONTEREY BAY, CALIFORNIA 72

A curious Gopher rockfish peers out of a crevice blanketed with Strawberry anemones. Decorator crabs (*Scyra acutifrons*) pick their way across the richly hued landscape. In the foreground is a Giant-spined sea star (*Pisaster giganteus*). The nutrient-rich cold waters along the coast of California support prolific growth and species diversity. Life covers every surface of the rocky subtidal reef in this scene beneath Monterey Bay.

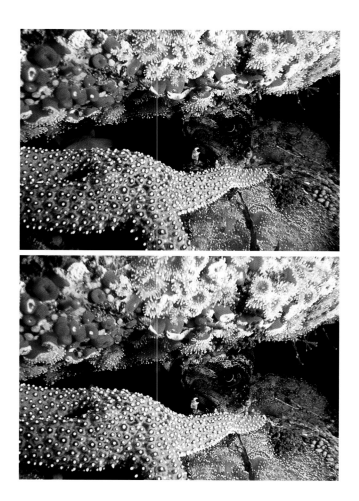

Tasseled Scorpionfish *SCORPAENOPSIS OXYCEPHALUS*

SIPADAN ISLAND, BORNEO, MALAYSIA

Most species in this large family are well camouflaged by flaps, tassels, and coloration matching the bottom terrain. Scorpionfish lie unseen in shallow waters, waiting motionlessly to swallow small fish. Some species also are nocturnal, sheltering in caves or rubble during the day. Although these secretive fish are well concealed, stereophotography helps to distinguish them from their hiding places— allowing for detailed but safe observation, since all scorpionfish have venomous spines and are considered dangerous. They are easy to set upon accidentally and should be regarded with caution.

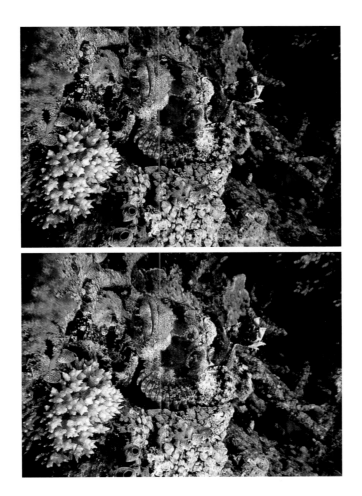

Splendid Toadfish *SANOPUS SPLENDIDUS*

COZUMEL ISLAND, MEXICO

This odd-shaped bottom dweller rests on its pectoral and ventral fins. It is common only to the island of Cozumel, off the Yucatan Peninsula of Mexico. A recluse, the toadfish hides in recesses or holes, as here, but may be photographed if approached slowly. Divers should be wary of the powerful jaws, however, which have crushed the fingers of more than one overly familiar underwater shutterbug. This specimen was located by following its unusual croaking sound.

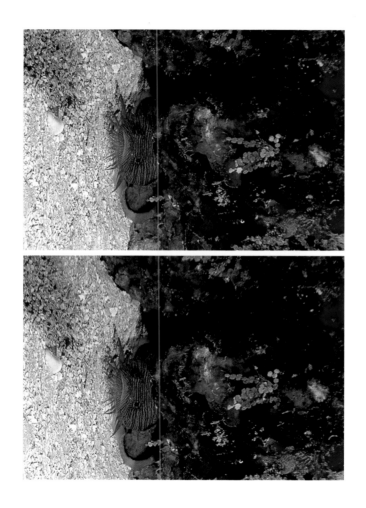

Longlure Frogfish *ANTENNARIUS MULTIOCELLATUS*

BONAIRE, NETHERLANDS ANTILLES, CARIBBEAN

The frogfish sits immobile on leglike pectoral fins, camouflaged on the sponge it so closely resembles. It has the ability to shift color through a variety of phases in order to blend into its surroundings. The frogfish's modified dorsal fin spine, almost invisible here, acts as a lure for unsuspecting fish. As a victim approaches the extended lure, the frogfish rapidly sucks the unsuspecting animal into a mouth cavity that can rapidly expand up to twelve times its normal volume.

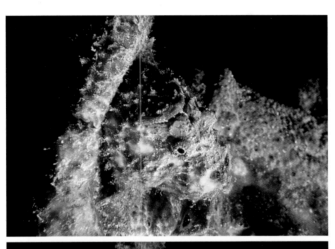

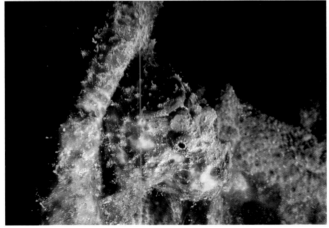

Spanish Shawl Nudibranch *FLABELLINOPSIS IODINEA*

MONTEREY BAY, CALIFORNIA

The purple and orange coloration of the Spanish shawl brilliantly advertises its presence to all nearby animals. Vivid color displays in nudibranchs are not accidental—they warn predators that the potential prey is unpalatable. Fish swallowing toxic nudibranchs quickly spit them out and learn to associate the animal's coloration with the unpleasant experience. However, not all predators are easily discouraged: The Navanax, another nearly shell-less marine snail, feeds voraciously on nudibranchs.

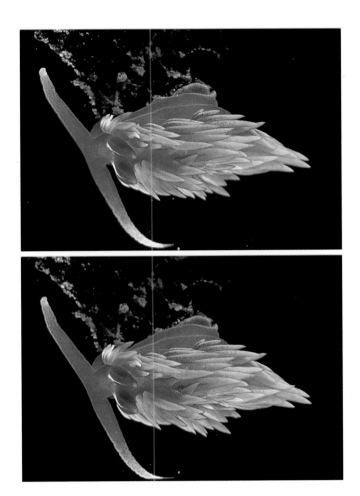

Coralline Sculpin *ARTEDIUS CORALLINUS*

POINT LOBOS STATE RESERVE, CARMEL BAY, CALIFORNIA

Like most sculpins, this small species matches the color of the algae on which it lives, Coralline algae. The female commonly lays eggs among the rocks, where they are guarded by the male. The strange, mucuslike filaments surrounding the fish in this photograph remain unexplained; however, other fish, such as certain parrotfish, secrete mucus cocoons believed to hide their scent from night-time reef predators.

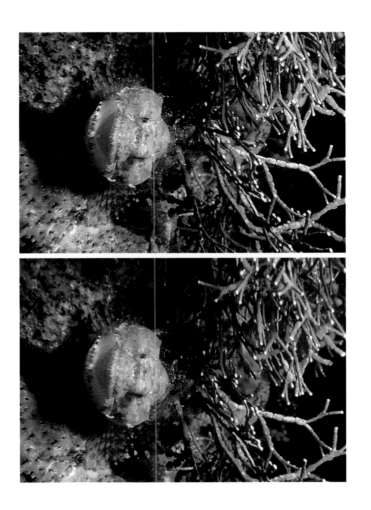

Anemone Crab *NEOPETROLISTHES OHSHIMAI*

SIPADAN ISLAND, BORNEO, MALAYSIA

Many aspects of the symbiotic relationship between the Anemone crab and the anemone have yet to be well studied. It is not understood whether the crab (and certain shrimp) must necessarily live with the anemone or can survive without the host. It is known that male and female crabs generally inhabit their host anemones in mated pairs. As with anemonefish, the crabs are immune to the stinging cells of the host anemone.

Bigeye Trevally

CARANX SEXFASCIATUS

SIPADAN ISLAND, BORNEO, MALAYSIA

Trevally and jacks are fast-swimming predators. Their tenacious character also makes them a favorite game fish. Trevally are open-water swimmers, or pelagic, but regularly visit reefs to feed on small fish and crustaceans. Adults are found individually or in schools and are easy to approach. The Bigeye trevally frequent seaward reef waters and channels, as seen here, off the face of a 2,000-foot dropoff at Sipidan Island.

Panamic Green Moray

GYMNOTHORAX CASTANEUS

SEA OF CORTEZ, MEXICO

Common in all tropical and semitropical seas, the nocturnal moray eel hides in crevices and caves by day. This is a typical scene, with the animal's head thrust out of a hole, mouth slowly opening and closing. At night the carnivorous moray ventures out over the reefs in search of prey. Its strong jaws, fanglike teeth, and leathery skin make it an extremely effective predator. Although divers can be seriously injured by the moray's lightning-fast strike, such attacks are normally reserved for divers foolish enough to put a hand into an eel's lair.

Coney *CEPHALOPHOLIS FULVUS*
on Orange Elephant Ear Sponge *AGELAS CALTHRODES*

COZUMEL ISLAND, MEXICO

This small member of the grouper family displays radically different colors and markings in three distinct color phases—reddish, bicolor, and golden. The Coney is hermaphroditic, beginning life as a female and maturing into a male. When photographed, this specimen was well concealed against the similarly colored and patterned Elephant ear sponge. But the camouflage effect is largely overcome by the combination of stereophotography and strobe lighting, which visually separate the fish from its background.

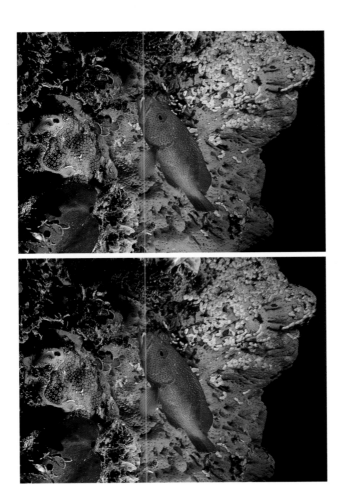

Glossary

An **aggregation** is the collection of many individuals into a group.

Algae (sing. alga) refers to a variety of single-celled and complex marine plants without true stems, leaves, or roots. Coralline algae form calcium carbonate crusts that are important in consolidating coral reefs.

Antennae are long, slender, flexible sensory organs located on the heads of insects and crustaceans.

Armor refers to an animal's protective outer layer.

Bivalves are animals (e.g., clams) that have a shell composed of two movable pieces.

Bottom-dwellers are organisms that live on the ocean floor and are not free-swimming.

Camouflage is a means of concealment by which something matches the appearance of its natural surroundings.

A **carapace** is a hard, bony, protective outer covering, such as the shell of a turtle or crab.

Carbon is an abundant nonmetallic element found in coal, limestone, petroleum, and other compound substances.

Chromatophores are pigment cells.

Class is a category used to classify animals.

Cleaning behavior is a special temporary relationship of mutual benefit between two animals. A larger animal (usually a fish) permits another, smaller animal (usually a fish or shrimp) to remove, or to clean, parasites and sloughing tissue from it.

Coelenterates are invertebrate organisms of the phylum Coelenterata (e.g., corals, sea anemones, jellyfish, sea fans, and hydroids). They are also called cnidarians.

Commensal refers to animals engaged in a symbiotic relationship with one another in which one animal depends on another without harming it.

Coral is the calcerous or horny skeletal deposit produced by polyps.

Crustaceans are mostly aquatic arthropods (including lobsters, shrimps, crabs, water fleas, and barnacles) that have a hard exoskeleton, a pair of appendages on each segment, and two pairs of antennae.

Defense mechanisms are behaviors an organism performs to protect itself from predators.

Exoskeleton refers to an animal's external supportive covering.

Gill covers are the flaps or lids that cover the gills or respiratory organs of marine animals.

Group is a term used to describe an assemblage of organisms when the degree or kind of relationship is not necessarily clear.

Gullet refers to the throat, where some animals take in food.

A **hierarchy** is a graded or ranked series, group, or set of groups.

The **host** is the larger, stronger, or dominant member of a symbiotic pair.

A **harem** is a group of females associated with one male.

Immunity refers to the ability to avoid or resist being harmed by certain diseases or toxins.

Incubation is the act or process of warming eggs by bodily heat to bring about the development of embryos and the hatching of young.

The **intertidal zone** is the area near or on shore, just above the low-tide mark.

An **invertebrate** is an animal that does not have a backbone (e.g., sponges, corals, jellyfish, shrimp, and sea cucumbers).

A **leviathan** is very large creature, as in a large sea animal or sea monster.

Macro stereophotography is the process by which three-dimensional photographs are taken of small-scale objects.

The **mantle** is the part of the body wall of a mollusk (e.g., clam, snail, nudibranch) that secretes the shell and encloses the animal's internal organs.

Medusa refers to a bell- or umbrella-shaped organism (e.g., jellyfish).

Mucous Cocoons are the protective outer coverings secreted by some marine animals.

Nematocysts are the stinging organs that coelenterates (e.g., sea anemones, corals, jellyfish, and hydroids) use to catch prey.

Nocturnal organisms are active mostly at night.

An **operculum bar** is a lid or flap that covers the gills of a fish.

A **parasite** is a living thing that spends its life on or in another organism, where it gets its food, often harming the host animal in the process.

Pelagic refers to organisms that are of the open ocean, free-swimming.

Pigment cells are cells that give coloring.

Plankton is the great host of plants and animals that drift in the sea's currents. Although some have the ability to swim (e.g., fish larvae), such movement is effective only on a small scale. All plankton are subject to the movement of ocean currents. "Zooplankton" refers to planktonic plants.

A **polyp** is an individual coelenterate (e.g., sea anemone, coral, jellyfish, sea fan, hydroid) which is attached to a surface, such as a rock, or to a colony of related animals. Its cylindrical body is usually closed and attached at one end, and open and free at the other end, where tentacles may surround a mouth.

A **predator** is an animal that captures and eats other animals.

Radula is the row of filelike teeth found in snails and other mollusks.

Rank is a social positioning of an organism based on any number of relative distinctions determined by the group within which it is organized.

A **reef** is a ridge of sand, a group of rocks, or a coral structure near the surface of water.

Schooling refers to a fish or aquatic animals swimming together in a large group.

Scuba [from self-contained underwater breathing apparatus] is an apparatus containing compressed air (or other gas mixtures) commonly used by divers.

Sequential hermaphroditism is a developmental process in which a dominant female, if there are no males in its territory, will change sex in order to assure continued breeding.

Sheltering is the act of fish or aquatic animals avoiding open water and swimming close to underwater formations, such as caves or reefs.

Siphon tubes are tubular organs in animals (esp. mollusks or arthropods) used for drawing in or ejecting fluids.

A **species** is a group of animals or plants that breed with one another and share similar physical characteristics.

A **spine** is a stiff, sharp-pointed growth on an animal or a plant.

A **sponge** is a marine lower invertebrate with an internal skeleton that is an elastic porous mass of interlacing horny fibers.

Symbiosis is a relationship in which an organism is closely associated with, and often depends upon, the life of another species.

Tentacles are long or short, fleshy, flexible appendages of an animal.

Territory is an area occupied and defended by an animal, often containing a nest site and food range.

A **toxin** is a poisonous substance.

Tunicates are a group of marine animals that outwardly resemble invertebrates, such as sponges and soft corals, but which in larval form reveal many characteristics shared with vertebrate, or "chordate" animals. As adults, they are generally attached to the sea bottom, although there are also planktonic forms.

A **vertebrate** is an animal that has a backbone or spinal column (e.g., fish, whales, humans).

Viscera (sing. viscus) are the internal organs of the body.

Acknowledgments

This book is dedicated to my wife, Marian, and my children, Ryan and Lauren. Without their loving support and patience, it would never have been possible. I wish to acknowledge my many friends in the Monterey Peninsula Underwater Photographers club, whose interest and enthusiasm have been an inspiration to me. For unfaltering technical support and friendship I am indebted to Dan Blodget of Sub Aquatic Camera Repair Company. Not least of all, I thank my sister Tanya for her editorial assistance, Mary Henness for processing all of my words, and my father for putting a camera in my hands at the right moment in my life.

About the author

Mark Blum combined three of his favorite hobbies—scuba diving, stereoscopic photography, and an interest in the natural world—when he took up underwater stereophotography in 1987. Though he picked up his first Stereo Realist camera at a neighbor's garage sale when he was 15, he has since designed most of his own equipment for 3-D underwater photography. With scuba gear and cameras in tow, he has travelled extensively, including trips to the Caribbean, Thailand, Malaysia, Indonesia, and Fiji. His unique work has won numerous awards, including Best of Show and other top awards in the National Stereoscopic Association, EPIC, Northern California Underwater Photographic Society, Seaviews, Los Angeles Underwater Photographic Society, and Innerspace competitions. He lives in Pacific Grove on Monterey Bay with his wife and two children.